CITIES OF THE
WORLD

SEATTLE

BY R. CONRAD STEIN

CP CHILDREN'S PRESS®
A Division of Scholastic Inc.
New York   Toronto   London   Auckland   Sydney
Mexico City   New Delhi   Hong Kong
Danbury, Connecticut

CONSULTANTS

John M. Findlay, Ph.D.
Department of History
University of Washington

Linda Cornwell
Learning Resource Consultant
Indiana Department of Education

Project Editor: Downing Publishing Services
Design Director: Karen Kohn & Associates, Ltd.
Photo Researcher: Jan Izzo

Library of Congress Cataloging-in-Publication Data
Stein, R. Conrad.
     Seattle / by R. Conrad Stein.
      p. cm. — (Cities of the world)
     Includes bibliographical references and index.
     Summary: Describes the history, culture, daily life, food, people, sports,
and points of interest in the largest city in the state of Washington.
     ISBN 0-516-20782-2 (lib.bdg.)   0-516-26463-X (pbk.)
     1. Seattle (Wash.)—Juvenile literature.   I. Title.
II. Series: Cities of the world (New York, N.Y.)
F899.S44S74 1999   98-45241
979.7'772—dc21   CIP
                                          AC

TABLE OF CONTENTS

THE SPACE NEEDLE

In 1962, the city of Seattle, Washington, hosted a grand World's Fair. Organizers of the fair wanted to build a memorable structure to serve as its focal point. So they erected the Space Needle. The Space Needle is a tower that is 605 feet (184 meters) tall with a revolving observation deck on top. The lofty tower, which represents high technology, is now the symbol of Seattle. It is a perfect emblem for this city that makes airplanes and spacecraft and designs computer software.

But ride the elevators to the top of the Space Needle and you will see a view of Seattle that has nothing to do with computers and the space age. On a clear day, you will be thrilled by a vista of lakes, rivers, the city's waterfront, and snowcapped Mount Rainier. Few other cities enjoy such gorgeous surroundings. Seattle is called the "Emerald City" because of its greenery and freshness. It is the largest city in the state of Washington. Seattle is also one of the most inviting cities in the world.

A fulll moon over the Seattle skyline with the Space Needle in the foreground

Visitors to the top of the Space
Needle (left) have a wonderful view
of Seattle and the surrounding area
including Mount Rainier (below).

A SECRET

Shhhh! Seattle, Washington, is a world-class city. It has fine theaters, parks, professional sports, industries that provide jobs, and great restaurants. But don't let anyone know about these wonders. If outsiders knew what an exciting city Seattle is, they'd flock here by the millions and spoil it for the rest of us. At least, that's what Seattle residents say.

THE SECRET IS OUT

In truth, Seattle was discovered long ago. The population of the metropolitan area now tops 3.5 million. Many citizens migrated to Seattle in recent years looking for a decent place to live. And—despite a few jokes about the newcomers—they were welcomed in this very friendly city.

Seattle has a rich ethnic mix. Whites hold a majority, African Americans make up roughly 8 percent of the population, and Asians about 13 percent. Hispanics and Native Americans are also part of the population. The various groups get along quite well. In 1989, Seattle elected its first African-American mayor, Norman B. Rice. Rice was elected despite the fact that only about one in ten voters was African American.

This girl is enjoying cotton candy at the annual Bite of Seattle food fair at the Seattle Center.

Most people agree that Seattle is a delightful city, but there is a common misunderstanding about its climate. Many outsiders say, "Yes, the streets are clean and the people seem happy. But it rains all the time." Wrong! Seattle averages about 37 inches (94 centimeters) of rain a year. Atlanta, Boston, New York, New Orleans, and a most of other cities have greater rainfall. However, Seattle's rain stretches over days and weeks. The rain comes in a fine mist rather than a downpour. In the winter months, a fog hangs over the city and gives the feeling that it is about to rain or that a strong rain has just ended. To Seattle residents, this condition of mist and near-rain is no big deal. Most carry an umbrella only on days when it rains hard enough to warrant using one. And residents dwell on the positives. Even in January, the temperature seldom dips below 35 degrees Fahrenheit (1.7° Celsius). Long, sunny days are common in the summer.

Umbrellas like this one (right) are opened on rainy days in Seattle (left).

A red footbridge in Kubota Gardens, a beautifully landscaped 20-acre (8-hectare) tract
designed by master landscaper Fujito Kubota and given by his estate to the city of Seattle

As is true with most big cities, Seattle does have problems. Everyone worries about rising crime even though statistics confirm that Seattle maintains a low crime rate compared to other urban areas. A more apparent problem rests in the hordes of homeless people. At least 3,000 people live on the streets of Seattle. Social workers say the number is much higher. The city's shelters cannot accommodate them all. Many homeless people are alcoholics or have drug addiction problems. They often create uncomfortable situations by begging in the streets. Some experts claim that Seattle's mild climate attracts homeless people from cities that have harsh winters.

Despite its problems, Seattle lives up to its nickname as the Emerald City. The popular maga-zine *Lear's* recently called Seattle "The Last Best City in America." *Money Magazine* hailed Seattle as "America's Most Livable City." So, the word is out. Seattle is a great place to live or to visit. But say it softly. Go along with the gag. Residents here still claim they want to hide this charming place from the rest of the world.

The International Fountain at Seattle Center

Skid Row, a Word Coined in Seattle

Every large city in the United States has at least one "Skid Row" neighborhood. Skid Row is usually an area of taverns and cheap hotels where day laborers and heavy drinkers gather. This rather low-life term was born in the Emerald City. Logging was one of Seattle's earliest industries. One sawmill built a long ramp, called a "skid road," which sped logs to the mill. Workers, and a few outright bums, hung around the ramp looking for temporary jobs. Eventually, the ramp and its rather unsavory surroundings was called "Skid Row." Thus, a new term entered the American vocabulary.

WATER, WATER EVERYWHERE

Colorful houseboats at the Gas Works Park Marina on Lake Union

These sightseers aboard a tour boat are viewing the Seattle skyline.

Look in the garage of the average Seattle home owner. In most, you will find a boat. According to statistics, one in six Seattle residents owns a boat. About 500 houseboats are docked in the Seattle area. Houseboat living was dramatized in the popular movie *Sleepless in Seattle*. Many homes are built on hills and have a picture window providing a sweeping view of a waterfront.

Seattleites are devoted to the water. And why not? On Seattle's waterfront (its front door) is Puget Sound. Puget Sound is a large inlet of the Pacific Ocean. The mighty Pacific lies about 125 miles (201 kilometers) west of the city. Within the city limits are Lake Union and Green Lake. To the east (Seattle's back door), spreads Lake Washington. The lake is 27 miles (43 km) long

Chittendon Locks (left), are part of the Lake Washington Ship Canal, which connects Puget Sound and Lake Washington.

The Seattle city skyline and the Bell Street Harbor Marina

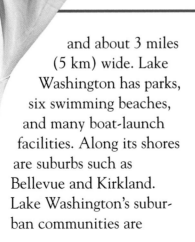

and about 3 miles (5 km) wide. Lake Washington has parks, six swimming beaches, and many boat-launch facilities. Along its shores are suburbs such as Bellevue and Kirkland. Lake Washington's suburban communities are generally called Seattle's Eastside.

Through the years, this wealth of water has enhanced Seattle's economy as well as its beauty. The city's setting on Puget Sound makes it a major port for oceangoing ships. Seattle was once called the Gateway to Alaska because it was the final refueling point for ships heading for Alaska's shores. The Lake Washington Ship Canal system (completed in 1917) allows boats to carry cargo from Puget Sound to Lake Washington.

Disks like these are used to store computer information.

THE PEOPLE AT WORK

Highway 405, popularly called the "Technology Corridor," runs through suburban Seattle. Some 250 computer companies are located on this highway. More than 60,000 computer technicians work in factories and offices along the Technology Corridor. Most of the technicians are young. Many are recent migrants to the Seattle area.

One of the brightest—and certainly the richest—of the computer people is Bill Gates. The son of a Seattle lawyer, Gates attended the city's Lakeside School. He began tinkering with computers when he was in the seventh grade. At the age of nineteen, Gates founded Microsoft. Today, Microsoft is the world's leading software company. From the beginning, Gates realized that software (programming) was more important for computer sales than hardware (the actual computers). The Microsoft Corporation has made Gates one of the wealthiest men in the world. His lakefront home in the suburb of Medina has a private movie theater and a dining room that seats 100 people.

Bill Boeing's first aircraft was an all-wood seaplane (above) that was used for airmail runs between Seattle and Vancouver, Canada. The picture at right shows Seattle's Boeing aircraft assembly plant.

The computer industry is the latest Seattle success story. Aviation has deeper roots in the city. In 1916, a wealthy Seattle lumberman named Bill Boeing developed a fascination for airplanes. He decided to build one. Appropriately for Seattle, Boeing's first craft was a seaplane. It had pontoons for landing on and taking off from water. The United States government was interested in Boeing's designs and gave him a small contract to make more planes. From this tiny beginning, an immense industry was born.

The Museum of Flight

Among the most popular museums in the Seattle area is the Museum of Flight, which is sponsored by the Boeing Company. Inside the museum, more than twenty full-size aircraft hang from the ceiling, giving the appearance of flight. World War I biplanes "fly" alongside sleek jets. Visitors can climb aboard the first presidential jet, *Air Force One*. Also part of the museum complex is the Red Barn, the Boeing Company's original building. The Red Barn dates to 1909.

During World War II (1939–1945), the Boeing Company concentrated on building huge, four-engine bombers. Two bombers—the B-17 and the B-29—made Boeing famous during the war years. After the war, Boeing led the aviation industry into the Jet Age. In the early 1950s, the company developed the 707. It was a four-engine jet plane that carried more than 100 passengers. Boeing now builds two-thirds of all the world's jet transport planes. One of its best-selling models is the giant 747. The 747 can fly 450 people nonstop about one-third of the way around the earth.

Today, Boeing dominates the world of Seattle business. It is estimated that one in every four people in the Seattle area works for Boeing or for its related industries. Yet it is a company that is heard but not seen. Boeing has no high-rise corporate headquarters building in downtown Seattle. Its biggest single plant is in the suburb of Everett, about an hour's drive north of downtown. Despite its seeming invisibility, Boeing's shift to the Jet Age changed the nature of the Seattle region.

During World War II, Seattle was a town of factory workers. Producing bombers required the efforts of thousands of men and women to assemble engines and rivet the skin onto aircraft frames. The beginning of jet production brought a gradual shift in the company's labor force. To manufacture large jet planes meant that more people were needed in the designers' offices than on the factory floor. Some 4 million parts go into the average 747. All these parts require special engineering and precisely drawn blueprints. During World War II, Boeing had three factory workers for every engineer and designer. In the Jet Age, that formula was reversed. Now, the vast majority of Boeing employees wear white collars rather than blue collars when they report to work.

The aircraft engineers, along with newly arriving computer technicians, strengthened Seattle's middle class. The modern Seattle region supports a large group of highly educated people who earn good money at work. They live in tidy neighborhoods and demand progressive schools for their children. Looking ahead to a world of high technology is no problem for youthful Seattleites. Few other cities face the future as confidently as does Seattle.

This exhibit in the Museum of Flight shows Flybaby *(above) and* Aerocar *(below), a shiny red sports car with wings.*

Near the south end of Seattle's waterfront is a charming neighborhood called Pioneer Square. It was here that Seattle began as an American city. By the 1960s, however, Pioneer Square had become a run-down section with many abandoned warehouses and factories. Plans were made to level the old buildings and create parking lots. "No!" said enraged Seattle citizens. So instead of being torn down, the buildings of Pioneer Square were carefully restored and fashioned into shops and offices. This rebirth of Pioneer Square is typical of Seattle. It is a young city by the standards of American history. But Seattle citizens are always mindful of their golden past.

THE BEGINNINGS

Washington and Oregon are part of a lovely region called the Pacific Northwest. The sea has always dominated the western side of this region. Hundreds of years ago, Native Americans who lived along the seacoast hunted whales from well-crafted canoes. The land's abundance allowed them to pursue the arts. Tribal masks, wood carvings, and other works of Native American art from the Pacific Northwest are now on display at the Seattle Art Museum.

The first European and American visitors to the Pacific Northwest came by sea. Fur traders led by English sea captain George Vancouver landed near Seattle in 1792. One of Vancouver's officers was named Puget, and Vancouver named Puget Sound in his honor. In 1841, American sea captain Charles Wilkes entered Puget Sound. Wilkes spotted an inlet and named it Elliott Bay, also after one of his crewmen. Elliott Bay later became the seaside gateway to Seattle.

The village that grew into Seattle was settled in 1852 by a group led by David and Arthur Denny of Illinois. Arthur Denny measured the depth of Elliott Bay in a unique manner. He took his wife's clothesline, tied a horseshoe to one end, and rowed about in a boat, dipping the line into the sea. Denny determined that Elliott Bay was deep enough to dock ships. He concluded that this wilderness site might very well become an important seaport.

The early settlers were greeted by Chief Sealth of the Suquamish and Duwamish tribes. He was described by the whites as being tall, handsome, and "a very friendly fellow." Chief Sealth urged some of the newcomers to build cabins on the grounds that now make up Pioneer Square. Chief Sealth (whose name was also pronounced Seattle) remained friendly with the settlers even after a short-lived war broke out between Native Americans and whites in 1856. White friends of the chief later named their village Seattle in his honor.

Totem poles like this one were made by Native Americans of the Pacific Northwest.

Puget Sound as it looked at the time of Seattle's settlement

Legacy of a Chief

Seattle grew so fast that Chief Sealth and his people were soon pushed out of their native lands. The chief died in 1866 and was buried in what is now the town of Suquamish, which lies across Puget Sound from downtown Seattle. Chief Sealth's story is sad. But his memory lives in many statues and paintings scattered around Seattle, his namesake town. The largest statue of Chief Sealth stands at Tillcum Place, at the intersection of Fifth Avenue and Denny Way.

CHIEF SEATTLE

PIONEER SEATTLE

In pioneer times, the Seattle area was covered by a magnificent forest. Douglas fir trees, 8 feet (2.4 m) thick at their bases, towered like great cathedrals over the land. It is no wonder that sawmills dominated industry in the early city. One sawmill was owned by Henry Yesler, who later became mayor. Yesler Way, a major downtown street, was named for that pioneer lumberman. Clearing the forests allowed the town to take shape. Today, however, one wishes the pioneers had the foresight to preserve at least a few groves of those marvelous trees.

The original settlement of Seattle as it looked in 1860 at what is now Pioneer Square

During the anti-Chinese riot
of 1886, at least five people
were shot and wounded.

The population of early Seattle was made up largely of white people from the eastern states. Also living in the village were recent immigrants from Germany and the Scandinavian countries. Many of these white people looked with alarm at Seattle's small but growing Chinese community. Laborers denounced the Chinese because they were willing to work for low wages. Even some churchmen accused the Chinese of bringing disease and filth to Seattle. In 1886, an anti-Chinese riot exploded in the city. Before the violence ended, at least five people were shot and wounded. Chinese-owned stores were looted. This ugly incident in the past stands in sharp contrast with modern Seattle. Today's city has a prosperous Asian community and generally enjoys racial harmony.

Scandinavian immigrants were
among Seattle's early settlers.
This girl is dressed in traditional
clothing for the city's Norway
Independence Day celebration.

By 1889, Seattle was a community of 25,000 people. Like most pioneer towns, it was made almost entirely of wood. In the downtown section, wooden buildings stood in long rows, almost touching one another. Streets and sidewalks were paved with wood planks. On the afternoon of June 6, a furniture builder on Front Street allowed a glue pot to boil over. A fire broke out in the furniture store and quickly spread to neighboring buildings. In less than an hour, the downtown core of Seattle was a sheet of roaring flames.

Miraculously, no one was killed in what history labeled Seattle's Great Fire. And the fire's almost total destruction allowed city leaders to rebuild with fire-resistant buildings and a more sensible plan. As work began, the *Seattle Post-Intelligencer* reported, "From the ruins will spring a new Seattle." The massive reconstruction energized the community with an attitude that was called the Seattle Spirit.

The Great Fire of 1889 destroyed the downtown core of Seattle.

Underground Seattle

One post-fire improvement was the raising of downtown streets to ease flooding. But building up the streets with gravel and dirt meant that stores were now one story or more below the sidewalks. Some merchants built stairs or even provided ladders so their customers could enter and buy goods. Most owners simply abandoned their old stores and built new shops at street level. This left a ghost town of old storefronts and sidewalks buried beneath the downtown streets. In the 1960s, a journalist named Bill Speidel began giving interesting and humorous tours of Seattle's old underground world. Today, tours of Underground Seattle remain popular with visitors.

Newspaper advertisements like this one drew thousands of people to the Yukon gold fields between 1900 and 1910.

"Gold!" "Gold!" These exciting words rang through the streets of Seattle in July 1897. A steamer called the *Portland* had just tied up at the docks carrying what one newspaper called "a ton of gold." The gold came from the Yukon area in Canada.

For the next few years, newcomers flocked into Seattle hoping to board ships, sail north, and strike it rich on Yukon gold. Largely because of the gold rush, the city's population skyrocketed from 81,000 to 237,000 between 1900 and 1910.

THE CUDAHY-HEALY YUKON-KLONDIKE MINING CO.

KLONDIKE GOLD FIELDS!

THE GREATEST INVESTMENT OF THE AGE!

A Chance for All to Come in on the Ground Floor.

THE CUDAHY-HEALY YUKON-KLONDIKE MINING CO.
Has been incorporated under the laws of the State of Montana, with a capital stock of $25,000,000, in 250,000 shares at $100 each, full paid and nonassessable. From this total of stock an amount equal to 20 per cent, or $5,000,000, has been set apart for development purposes, and upon these 50,000 shares a dividend of 5 per cent upon the par value is guaranteed to be paid out of the profits of each year before any dividends are paid for that year upon the balance; then the balance to receive any dividend up to 5 per cent and then the remaining dividend earned to be payable on the whole $25,000,000, and these guaranteed shares are now offered to the public for immediate investment **AT THIRTY-FIVE DOLLARS ($35) PER SHARE,** at which price the **GUARANTEED DIVIDEND** will be over **14 PER CENT** on the investment

PROPERTY.	PROSPECTS.	PURPOSES.
The company's general property consists of lands, mines and mining equipment in the valley of the Yukon River and on its tributary streams in Alaska and the British Northwest Territory. The mineral beds owned include Gold, in placer and quartz claims, Silver, Copper and Coal, their chief locations being on the Tananah River, Miller, Birch, Forty-Mile and Sixty-Mile Creeks, Klondike River, Too Much Gold Creek, Bonanza, Boulder and Eldorado Creeks.	There is ample evidence before the public of the wonderful wealth of Gold along the Yukon and Klondike basins. The company owns large numbers of gold placer and quartz claims, selected by its experts out of many hundreds during five years of patient prospecting. Claim No. 3 on Miller Creek, from which over $100,000 was taken last year, is now a part of the property of this company, and is in operation; Copper prospects are on the Tananah River and are very rich. Very extensive and rich Coal beds near Cudahy, 1,000 acres in area, are to be opened at once. The contract has already been let for 20,000 tons of this coal at $4.00 per ton.	Heavy immigration of mining labor into the Yukon Valley, which is now going on, is what is needed for the development of this mineral wealth. Work will begin next Spring on as many of the placers as possible. At all these points in the near vicinity of the claims, are stores and trading posts of the North American Transportation and Trading Company. Our officers and directors are also interested in the management of this company, insuring hearty co-operation.

This Company does not have to prospect for property— It already owns it.   Some of its mines are now in operation.

CAUTION:
The Cudahy-Healy Yukon-Klondike Mining Company has no occasion whatever to color or exaggerate its advantages. CAPTAIN JOHN J. HEALY of Dawson City, Northwest Territory, has had forty years' experience in prospecting and mining in Idaho, Montana, Black Hills and the Rocky Mountains, and every statement here given is strictly conservative. Keep your eye on our treasure steamers "Portland" and "Cleveland," which are bringing in the gold on every trip.

Officers of the Cudahy-Healy Yukon-Klondike Mining Co.

JOHN CUDAHY, Chicago, Ill., President.
CAPTAIN JOHN J. HEALY, Yukon River, Alaska; and Dawson, N. W. T., Manager.

ELI A. GAGE, Chicago, Ill., and Yukon River, Alaska, Secretary.
WILLIAM W. WEARE, Chicago, Ill, Treasurer.

DIRECTORS.

CAPTAIN JOHN J. HEALY, Yukon River, Alaska; and Dawson, N. W. T.
JOHN CUDAHY, Chicago, Ill.
SENATOR T. C. POWERS, Helena, Mont.
CHARLES A. WEARE, Chicago, Ill.
PORTUS B. WEARE, Chicago, Ill.
CHARLES WEARE, Cedar Rapids, Ia.

ELY E. WEARE, Dawson, N. W. T.
Fort Cudahy, N. W. T.
WILLIAM W. WEARE, Chicago, Ill.
HENRY G. WEARE, Black Hills, Spearfish, S. Dak.
JOHN WEARE, Chicago, Ill.

Bankers—CORN EXCHANGE BANK, Chicago, Ill., U. S. A.
BANK OF MONTREAL, Chicago, Ill., U. S. A.

☞ Subscriptions for stock received in person or by letter at Room 293, Old Colony Building, Chicago, Ill., and 303 Produce Exchange, New York City.

Buy One Share at once. If you have not $35.00 club with your friends. Shares will undoubtedly soon increase in value. This company has many times superior opportunities to make money than any other company possibly can have.

TWENTIETH-CENTURY SEATTLE

Some visitors complain that modern Seattle is too hilly. But in the old days, the hills were so steep that horses pulling streetcars often got too tired to lug the cars up a grade. When that happened, passengers had to get off and help push the streetcar. After the turn of the century, many hills were flattened out. Workers used high-pressure water hoses to wash them away. With the worst of the hills gone, the city was free to expand even more rapidly than it had in the past.

Again, Seattle's key position by the sea contributed to its growth. In 1909, a great fair called the Alaska-Yukon-Pacific Exposition was held on the University of Washington campus near Lake Washington. The fair drew more than 3 million people. The opening of the Panama Canal in 1914 also benefited Seattle's shipping interests. The Panama Canal halved the travel time between eastern ports and Seattle. The Lake Washington Ship Canal, which linked Lake Washington with Puget Sound, was completed in 1917.

During World War II, ships and planes were produced in Seattle. Prosperity

This photograph of Seattle's Second Avenue was taken about 1900.

continued in the postwar period. The 1962 Century 21 Exposition drew millions of visitors and left the city with a host of new structures: the Space Needle, the Pacific Science Center, the Opera House, and the Playhouse. In the late 1960s, Boeing experienced a slump in sales and laid off two-thirds of its workers. Because of the troubles at Boeing, one in every six Seattleites was unemployed.

By the 1980s, Boeing had recovered from its slump. Also, computer companies opened in the suburbs, making the Seattle area less dependent on the aviation industry. People from all over the country were beginning to discover the charms of Seattle. Droves of newcomers moved to the Emerald City. At the same time, many Seattleites migrated to the suburbs. Consequently, the population of Seattle proper (within the city limits) decreased slightly from 1960 to 1980. However, the population of Greater Seattle (including the suburbs) almost doubled. By 2000, the city of Seattle held just a half million people while Greater Seattle was home to more than 3.5 million.

President William Howard Taft (left) officially opened the Alaska-Yukon-Pacific Exposition (below) in 1909.

Seattle is many things to many people, but it is never boring to anyone. There are endless activities here—shopping, sports, music, theater, and the arts. It is no mystery why the population of the Seattle area keeps growing. People want to move here to enjoy living in an exciting setting.

SPORTS

On fall Saturdays, some 74,000 Seattleites crowd into Husky Stadium at the University of Washington. The university itself is a cherished Seattle institution. It was founded in Seattle in 1861, and now serves 35,000 students and 16,500 teachers and staff. Seattleites cheer when the school's football team, the Huskies, wins. Former players are legends. The Huskies' powerful running back Hugh McElhenny, who played during the 1950s, is still a hero to older Seattle fans. For generations, the Huskies were the city's main show in spectator sports.

In 1967, the SuperSonics, a National Basketball Association (NBA) team, was established in Seattle. Professional football and baseball arrived soon after the SuperSonics. The pro teams made Seattle a "Major League" city. In 1979, the SuperSonics won the NBA crown, and the celebrations lasted for days. The teams have given the city genuine sports heroes. Gary Payton is the SuperSonics' premier player of the 1990s. On defense, Payton sticks so close to his opponent he is nicknamed "The Glove." Ken Griffey Jr. is the Seattle Mariners' baseball superstar. Griffey is a rare package of speed, power hitting, and superb fielding.

The Washington Huskies' logo

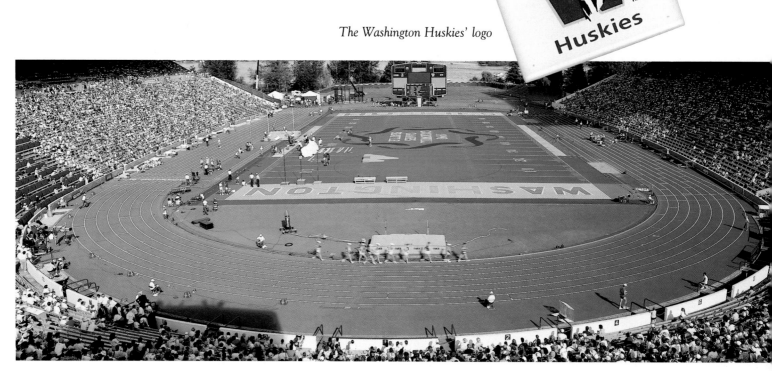

The Huskies play college football at the University of Washington's Husky Stadium.

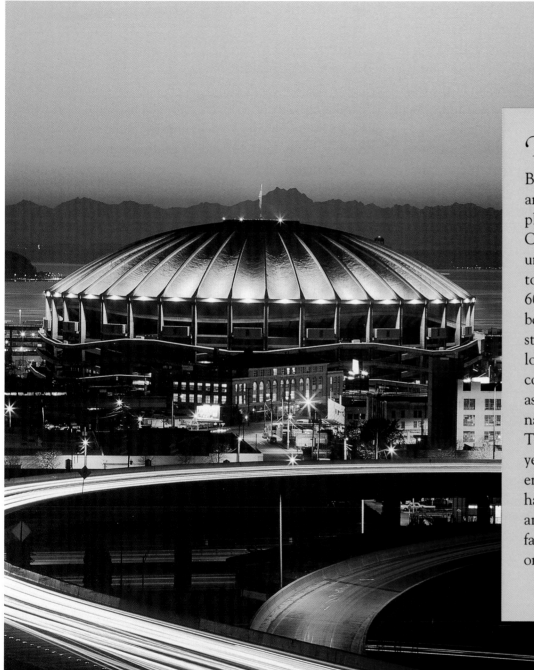

The Kingdome

Both the Mariners (baseball) and the Seahawks (football) play in Seattle's Kingdome. Completed in 1976, the stadium holds up to 66,000 spectators for football and about 60,000 for baseball. It also boasts the world's largest free-standing roof. Its downtown location makes the stadium convenient for residents as well as fans. But rapid change is the nature of professional sports. Though the Kingdome is not yet thirty years old, team owners, city officials, and voters have decided to tear it down and build two new outdoor facilities—one for baseball and one for football and soccer.

Spectator sports are just one element of Seattle's sporting life. Seattleites are a vigorous people who enjoy hiking, bicycling, and mountain climbing. The city is nearly surrounded by water, making water sports a special lure.

Experts claim there are 150 species of fish in Puget Sound and 35 species in Lake Washington. The greatest prizes for anglers are steelhead and salmon. If you don't fancy catching fish, you can always watch them swim for their lives at Seattle's Fish Ladder. At spawning time fish are driven by instinct to return to their birthplaces. Each year, a half million fish swim, jump, and fight their way upstream at the Fish Ladder, which links Puget Sound with Lake Washington. Spectators watch their plight from above the Fish Ladder or through six lighted viewing windows along the sides. Children like to cheer on the smaller fish as they gallantly swim against the strong current.

On summer days, Seattle's lakes and waterfront are filled with pleasure boats. Sailboats bend to catch breezes. Huge powercraft break the waves. A grand parade of boats flows over Puget Sound during Seafair, a city festival held every August. A highlight of Seafair is a very noisy race of hydroplanes. Hydroplanes are streamlined motorboats that skim across the top of the water and reach speeds of 200 miles (322 km) per hour. The Seafair festival is so popular that the city's Japanese-American community holds its Bon Odori party at the same time. The party features Japanese dancing, drumming, and foods.

Salmon like this one swim up Seattle's Fish Ladder every year at spawning time.

Most Seattleites love outdoor
sports, including hiking, bicycling,
and mountain climbing.
These cyclists and hikers (left) are
on the Burke-Gilman Trail.
The mountain climbers (below) are
challenging Mount Rainier.

Discovery Park (left), the largest
park in Seattle, has miles of
beaches and trails.

Boys playing soccer at a downtown Seattle park

*Inline skating is a popular
activity in Seattle parks.*

Parks are outdoor gymnasiums in Seattle. In the parks, people engage in inline skating, bicycling, and skateboarding. Seattle has 300 parks and playgrounds and more than 5,000 acres (2,023 hectares) of parkland. At 527 acres (213 ha), Discovery Park is Seattle's largest. Discovery Park has trails that wind through thick forests and 2 miles (3 km) of beaches. A wild cougar was seen at Discovery Park in 1982. Downtown's Freeway Park is an oasis of nature in the bustle of the city. Alki Beach reminds many visitors of southern California. During the summer, Alki Beach is a magnet for bikini-clad teenagers and suntanned volleyball players.

Bikes are seen everywhere in Seattle. Recently, *Bicycling Magazine* called Seattle "America's number one city for biking." Streets have "bikes only" lanes, and there are dozens of trails designed for bicycling. A popular bicycle run is the Burke-Gilman Trail, which runs 12 miles (19 km) from Gas Works Park on Lake Union to Logboom Park on Lake Washington. The trail, which was built over abandoned railroad tracks, has more than 1 million users each year.

Hiking and backpacking might very well be the most popular sports among Seattle residents. According to some estimates, as many as a quarter million Seattleites regularly hike in the mountains outside their city. The Sammamish River Trail, which winds 27 miles (43 km) through beautiful river scenery, is especially favored among hikers.

THE MUSIC SCENE

A street musician at Westlake Center

In the late 1940s, jazz pianist Ray Charles lived in Florida trying to make money through his music. He found few paying jobs. Charles, who is blind, asked a friend to look at a map and select a city as far from Florida as he could get. The friend pointed to Seattle, and Charles took a train to the Emerald City. There, in downtown jazz clubs, Ray Charles found an audience for his special music and songs. From his Seattle base, Charles became a legendary figure in jazz.

While performing in the Emerald City, Charles met Seattle native Quincy Jones. Jones was a talented trumpet player. He joined Ray Charles's jazz band. A brilliant arranger, Quincy Jones is today a top producer of rhythm and blues music. Another musician from the Seattle area was Jimi Hendrix. Many rock fans call Hendrix the "Father of the Electric Guitar." Interestingly, Ray Charles, Quincy Jones, and Jimi Hendrix are all African Americans. Yet these three black musicians rose to fame performing before Seattle's mostly white fans.

In the late 1980s, a new sound—grunge—swept Seattle. It was a defiant form of music. Some say grunge is protest music for white youngsters, while rap is the call to rebellion for young African Americans. Fans of grunge are characterized by their baggy shorts and backward baseball caps. Rock purists complain that the music is overly loud and too rough—"You know, it sounds . . . grungy." Nevertheless, grunge groups such as Nirvana, Soundgarden, and Mudhoney rose to stardom in the 1990s. And grunge lovers can thank Seattle for the birth of their special sound.

Many music historians believe Seattle is an ideal launching ground for new movements and budding performers. They cite the success of grunge and the keen audiences who were the first to appreciate the talent of a jazz performer such as Ray Charles. A fresh musical style is embraced more readily here than it would be in New York or Los Angeles. Seattle is a place where a young musician can take risks.

The Emerald City offers a wide variety of music certain to appeal to all tastes. Classical music lovers attend performances given by the Seattle Symphony Orchestra, the Seattle Opera, and the Seattle Youth Symphony. The University of Washington School of Music also presents classical symphonies and chamber music. A special group called the Sea-Chordsmen is devoted to preserving barbershop quartet songs. The Ladies Musical Club of the University of Washington gives regular choral concerts. Seattle's ethnic communities enrich the music scene with organizations such as the Norwegian Male Chorus and the Cape Fox Dancers (a Native American group).

A participant in the Japanese Drum Ceremony in Seattle's International District

Young girls dance at the Seafair Powwow, held at the Daybreak Star Indian Cultural Center.

39

SHOPPING, BROWSING, AND THE LIKE

Nordstrom is now a chain of department stores with locations throughout the country. It began as a Seattle shoe store. Nordstrom is one of many successful businesses born in Seattle. Shopping is always a fun experience in the Emerald City. Seattle has suburban malls as well as neighborhood flea markets. In north Seattle, the Northgate Mall opened in 1950 as one of the very first shopping malls in the United States. Serving 500,000 people a week, Northgate is still the most widely used shopping mall in the city. Seattle also has an old market where shopping is a very different adventure from the malls.

The Pike Place Market began in 1907 when a dozen or so farmers gathered at Pike Place and Stewart Street to sell vegetables from their horse-drawn wagons. The market now spills over a complex of buildings near the waterfront. Its smells, sounds, and color give the Pike Place Market a special form of energy. Fish sellers hold huge flounder and salmon over their heads to lure customers. T-shirt vendors will put any message on a shirt for a small fee. Newspaper hawkers shout out headlines. As many as 40,000 shoppers visit this madcap marketplace every day.

You can walk to the Pike Place Market by going through Victor Steinbrueck Park. Here stand two Pacific Northwest totem poles designed by a member of the Quinault tribe. But the real attractions at Steinbrueck are the street entertainers. Most of them are licensed. The city issues about 300 street entertainment licenses a year. A classical music trio performs there regularly. So does a man who wheels his own piano around. A woman gospel singer is a favorite regular performer.

A fish vendor at Pike Place Market shows off his wares.

This Pike Place Market shop has fresh raspberries and blueberries for sale.

The Coffee Lovers

Seattleites are crazy about European-style espresso coffee. Espresso is not simply brewed and poured from a pot. It is very strong coffee made by quickly forcing a small amount of very hot water through dark-roasted, finely ground coffee beans. Coffee houses serving espresso abound in Seattle. Vendors with pushcarts sell coffee on downtown streets. The city's favorite is café latte, an espresso drink served with steamed milk. As far as anyone can remember, the first espresso cart appeared downtown in 1980. Now there are dozens of carts and espresso restaurants scattered throughout the city. Seattle is truly daffy over coffee.

Right: A Chinese restaurant in Seattle's International District

Below: A selection of sushi, a specialty served by many Japanese restaurants in the International District

Shoppers get hungry. No problem. Stop for lunch at Seattle's International District. A compact neighborhood near downtown, it has long been the home of immigrants from Asia. Now it is a delightful center of Chinese, Japanese, and Filipino restaurants. Try a Japanese specialty such as sushi. Try lemon chicken at a Chinese restaurant. Koreans, Vietnamese, and Cambodians are among the newest immigrants to the International District, and their restaurants add to the spicy variety of the neighborhood. Some travelers rate Seattle as one of the best cities for Asian foods in the United States.

These outdoor diners are enjoying a summer evening on South Lake Union.

ENVIRONS

Seattle and its suburbs have a wealth of museums, parks, shops, theaters, and other points of interest. Beyond the Seattle area lie stunning natural wonders. An exciting urban setting blended with the nearby gifts of nature make Seattle unique among the world's cities.

SEATTLE PROPER

The Kingdome stands in downtown Seattle. When there are no games taking place, guests can take tours of this massive domed stadium. Inside is a museum holding items of sports memorabilia, including a pair of former heavyweight champion Muhammad Ali's boxing shorts. Near the Kingdome is the Klondike Gold Rush Museum, where photos and exhibits recall the Yukon and Alaskan Gold Rushes of the 1890s and early 1900s. Gold fever struck the town in those days. Thousands of Seattleites headed to the Yukon, driven by dreams of wealth. As the exhibits point out, only a scant few struck it rich.

The Columbia SeaFirst Center, which rises 76 stories, is Seattle's tallest building. However, Seattleites frequently criticize its unimaginative glass-and-steel design. The most beloved of Seattle's high-rise buildings is Smith Tower, built in 1914. When completed, the 42-story Smith Tower was hailed as the tallest building in the West. For generations, it was Seattle's most prominent landmark. Smith Tower remains precious in the hearts of older residents.

Seattle clings to its Native American heritage. In Pioneer Square stands a totem pole built in Alaska by Tlingit Indian craftsmen. Near the totem pole is a bust of Chief Sealth. At Cherry and Second Street is a plaque marking this as the site of the first cabin built by a white man in this city. Just off Pioneer Square spreads Waterfall Park. This is a fine place to take a break and watch water tumble

A detail of the Tlingit Indian totem pole that stands in Pioneer Square

Waterfall Park, just off Pioneer Square, is a pleasant place for tired sightseers to take a restful break.

An exhibit of mining tools and supplies in the Klondike Gold Rush Museum

over an artificial falls. Some blocks away, visitors find the Seattle Art Museum. Featured in the museum are artworks by Native Americans, African Americans, and artists native to the Pacific Northwest.

The International District is more than a col-

lection of Asian restaurants and shops. It is also a vibrant community of hardworking people.

Tucked between apartment buildings in the district are vegetable gardens that are carefully tended by the residents. Chinese opera, complete with bells and gongs, is performed at

the neighborhood's Luck Ngi Musical Club. The Wing Luke Asian Museum is devoted to the history of Asian immigrants in America. Asian people have lived in this neighborhood since the very beginning of Seattle. A tea store owned by a Mr. Wa Chung opened on the cor-

ner of Third and Washington in 1871. At the time, the tea store was only the third brick structure in the city.

Lying just below the Space Needle is the Pacific Science Center. Here are robots, dinosaurs, and the Imax Theater with a screen taller than a house. The Science Center's Tech Zone is especially popular with children. Young guests are invited to don helmets and play virtual basketball or hang glide over a virtual city. Along the waterfront, the Seattle Aquarium is a "window" to the marine life of Puget Sound. In pens are frolicking sea otters. A fascinating variety of Puget Sound fish swim in glass cases.

Parks dot the communities north of downtown. Woodland Park is home to the Woodland Park Zoo. Visitors at the zoo walk its "trails." The Northern Trail leads past river otters, brown bears, timber wolves, and other animals typical of the north woods. The Trail of Vines takes one into an Asian rain forest where monkeys scurry through trees and exotic birds call to each other. Green Lake Park encircles the lovely Green Lake. It is said you are not a true Seattleite until you have hiked, biked, or skated around Green Lake at least once. Gas Works Park was once the home of a polluting factory complex that produced gas for industry. Some of the gas tanks and machinery remain, but the 20-acre (8-ha) site is now one of the city's most popular parks.

Five life-size robotic whales move around this pool at the Pacific Science Center.

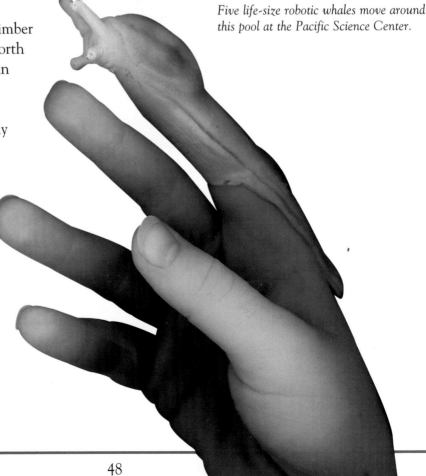

Tree slugs are a common sight in Washington, especially in parks and forest preserves. This child is wearing a tree slug finger puppet.

An array of blossoming roses in the Woodland Park Rose Garden

Take the Bus

To get around downtown, one should take the bus. Believe it or not, the ride is free. Between 6:00 A.M. and 7:00 P.M., all downtown buses operate at no cost to the riders. Seattle is protective of its environment. Offering free bus service cuts down on car traffic and, therefore, reduces air pollution.

EASTSIDE SEATTLE

On the eastern shores of Lake Washington are the towns of Kirkland, Redmond, Bellevue, and Mercer Island. This collection of suburbs is called the Eastside. The towns began more than 100 years ago as farming and fishing communities. They have grown at an astonishing rate in recent years, but each retains its own traditions and a separate personality.

Years ago, a family drive from Bellevue to downtown Seattle meant packing a lunch because the car had to go around the 27-mile (43-km)-long Lake Washington. Today, two "floating" bridges span the lake. The bridges are constructed in such a way that their main spans float on the lake's surface.

Colorful playground equipment attracts children to Bellevue's many excellent city parks.

However, the Eastside is a victim of its own popularity. So many people and businesses have moved to the Eastside that traffic jams on the bridges can slow a car trip to almost the pre-bridge time.

Kirkland is a town of about 45,000 people. It has grassy lakefront parks and excellent seafood restaurants. The Kirkland Creative Arts Center offers painting and sculpture classes to adults and to children. Kirkland's population expanded so fast after World War II that it contributed to the growth of a neighboring suburb, Redmond.

Since 1970, Redmond's population has tripled to reach 45,256. Redmond is the world headquarters for the Microsoft Corporation. A popular attraction in Redmond is the Marymoor Velodrome, a banked course where the country's best bicyclists come to race.

Bellevue was once a sleepy small town. Today, it is the state of Washington's fifth-largest city. Along Bellevue's waterfront stand some of the richest homes in the Seattle area. Shops and restaurants in Bellevue are known for their elegance. Its huge mall, Bellevue Square, contains more than 200 stores. Teenage mall walkers call visiting Bellevue Square "squaring off." Bellevue also boasts excellent city parks. The 37-acre (15-ha) Bellevue Botanical Gardens contain exotic shrubs, a pond, and a waterfall.

Mercer Island has few shopping centers or industries. Residents like it that way. Relatively light traffic makes the streets of Mercer Island safe for bicyclists. The 77-acre (31-ha) Luther Burbank Park is a haven for bike riders. Now a community of 22,036 people, the island was once a summer home for Seattle's middle class. At that time, it could be reached only by ferryboat. Today, the Mercer Island Floating Bridge links the island with the mainland. In many ways, the Mercer Island community typifies Seattle: a people surrounded by water.

Waterfront recreation at Luther Burbank Park on Mercer Island

OUTLYING WONDERS OF NATURE

Cross Puget Sound from Seattle and you enter a different world. West of the metropolitan area is Bainbridge Island and the Kitsap Peninsula. Here, suburbs and farming and fishing villages prevail. Life moves at a slower pace in those communities than it does in Seattle. The town of Poulsbo is nicknamed "Little Norway" because of its resemblance to a Norwegian fishing village. Nearby is the burial site of Chief Sealth. The seashore here is windswept, wild, and has changed very little over the centuries.

Rising west of the Kitsap area is the Olympic Peninsula. It is a place where the sea and the mountains meet in a lovely marriage. In 1888, the territorial governor of Washington visited here and wrote in awe, "The mountains seem to rise from the edge of the water, as though nature had designed to shut up this spot for her safe keeping forever." In the center of the peninsula are Mount Olympus and

Petroglyphs (rock carvings) on a beach in Olympic National Park

This hiker is enjoying a view of the Olympic Mountains.

Olympic National Park. The park covers 900,000 acres (364,221 ha). Some 600 miles (966 km) of hiking trails lead guests through groves of old-growth fir trees. Many of those trees are as tall as 10-story office buildings. Along the park's Hoh River stands a haunting rain forest where junglelike mosses cover the trees.

Club moss up to 3 feet (90 cm) long festoons this fallen log in Olympic National Park's Hoh Rain Forest.

Seattle's Famous Ferryboats

Ferryboats regularly leave the Seattle waterfront for trips into Puget Sound. They are part of the Washington State Ferry system, which serves 23 million riders a year. Passengers include regular commuters as well as vacationers. From the deck, a ferryboat passenger will see snow-capped mountains, the stunning skyline of Seattle, and perhaps even a few Orca whales leaping through the waters.

A wooden model of a Washington State Ferry

East of Seattle stands the Cascade Mountain Range. In the Cascades are Mount Rainier and Mount Baker, two of the tallest peaks in North America. On clear days, the snow-capped top of Mount Rainier can be seen from downtown Seattle. Thousands of Seattleites take the two-hour drive to Mount Rainier National Park. The mountain presents a challenge to serious hikers. Climbers can follow

Mount Baker, in the Cascade Mountains, is one of the tallest peaks in North America.

trails up the face of the mountain. Backpackers can trek the 93-mile (150-km) Wonderland Trail, which encircles Mount Rainier.

After a trip to Mount Rainier, tourists return to Seattle. The towering Space Needle begins and ends many visits to this lovely city by the sea. Having seen Seattle in its glorious natural setting, it is easy for visitors to understand why it is called the Emerald City.

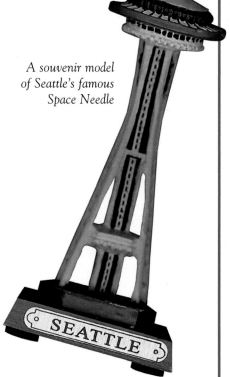

A souvenir model of Seattle's famous Space Needle

Background: A view of Mount Rainier from Paradise Meadows
Inset: A mother and daughter try to coax deer to come close on a trail near Paradise Meadows.

FAMOUS LANDMARKS

The Hammering Man statue outside the Seattle Art Museum

A fish market in the International District

Waterfront Park

The Waterfront
Home of Waterfront Park and Seattle's many piers. Pier 51 is the Seattle Ferry Terminal. Docking here is a fleet of 25 oceangoing ferryboats that carry 23 million passengers and 10 million cars each year.

Pioneer Square
Seattle began here some 150 years ago. The historic district almost met the wrecking ball in 1966 when plans were made to tear down the old buildings to create parking lots. But Seattle residents would not allow the neighborhood to be razed. Today, Pioneer Square is an 88-acre (36-ha) expanse of offices, restaurants, and specialty shops.

The International District
Known for its Asian shops and restaurants, this is also a close-knit neighborhood of hardworking people. Asian Americans have lived in this district for more than 100 years.

Smith Tower
At 42 stories, Smith Tower (completed in 1914) was once the tallest building west of the Mississippi River. Today, it is not even among the top-ten tallest structures that rise over the city's skyline. Still, the landmark building is beloved by Seattleites, especially the older residents.

The Space Needle
Built for the 1962 Century 21 Exposition, the structure is now the supreme symbol of Seattle. Visitors take the Space Needle's elevator up 600 feet (183 m) to the observation deck. The elevator ride takes a stomach churn-ing 43 seconds. On top are restaurants and shops. The floor turns one complete revolution every hour.

The Pacific Science Center
A complex of six interconnected buildings, this science museum is a hit with children. Most exhibits are hands-on. Models include dinosaurs, whales, and many other attractions. The Pacific Science Center stands in a 74-acre (30-ha) parklike set-ting called the Seattle Center.

Gold nuggets on display at the Klondike Gold Rush Museum

Below left: The city skyline and Mount Rainier
Below: The Pacific Science Center

The Monorail
The futuristic monorail train whisks people from downtown to the Seattle Center in about 90 seconds. Riding it is a must for visitors.

The Klondike Gold Rush Museum
This museum's official name is the Klondike Gold Rush National Historic Park. But it is, in fact, a storefront museum dedicated to the 1897 Yukon Gold Rush that contributed so greatly to Seattle's growth. Old photos displayed here allow guests to discover the thrills of Seattle's history.

The Seattle Art Museum
This 5-story, $27-million building houses works of art from around the world. Prized pieces include Japanese tomb art dating back 4,000 years.

Volunteer Park
The park was named after Seattle residents who volunteered to fight in the Spanish-American War of 1898. Its highlight is a conservatory, built in 1912, which holds a colorful collection of orchids, lilies, and passionflowers.

Seattle Asian Art Museum
Once the old Seattle Art Museum, the building was reopened in 1994 and dedicated to Asian art. It is now the pride of the city's sizable Asian-American community and holds paintings and sculptures from China, Japan, Korea, India, and other Asian countries.

Green Lake
This large and sparkling lake lies within the city limits and is completely encircled by parkland. It is a center for jogging, bicycling, and family fun in Seattle. The attached Woodland Park has a popular zoo.

The Museum of History and Industry
Seattle's history museum allows visitors to imagine Seattle as it looked 100 years ago. Photographs, toys, old tools, and other items take guests on a journey to the city's past.

FAST FACTS

POPULATION 2000

Seattle	563,374
Metropolitan Area	3,554,760

LAND AREA 84 square miles (218 sq km)

LOCATION Seattle is in the state of Washington, along Puget Sound. It is 113 miles (182 km) south of the Canadian border and 125 miles (201 km) east of the Pacific Ocean. The land region surrounding Seattle is generally called the Pacific Northwest.

LAND PROFILE Seattle is virtually surrounded by water. To the west is Puget Sound and to the east is the long and narrow Lake Washington. The Lake Washington Ship Canal allows ship passage between Lake Washington and Puget Sound. Within the city are Lake Union and Green Lake. To the east are the Cascade Mountains, which include the towering Mount Rainier. On a clear day, the peak of Mount Rainier can be seen from the city.

CLIMATE Mild weather allows Seattleites to play sports and enjoy outdoor activities the year round. In July, high temperatures average about 75° Fahrenheit (24° Celsius). In winter, the temperature falls below freezing only about 15 days a season. Though Seattle is thought of as a rainy city, it actually has less total rainfall a year than Chicago. In Seattle, however, rain comes in drizzles and mists that stretch over days and weeks rather than in brief downpours.

INDUSTRIES The aviation industry, led by the giant Boeing Company, is the Seattle area's leading business. Also located in greater Seattle is Microsoft, the world's largest maker of software for personal computers. Other manufactured goods produced in the Seattle area include outdoor recreational clothing and equipment, electrical machinery, toys, and shoes. The fishing industry is also active. Seattle's port handles 20 million short tons (18 million metric tons) of freight each year.

CHRONOLOGY

1792
English sea captain George Vancouver lands near Seattle and names Puget Sound after one of his officers.

1841
Charles Wilkes, an American mariner, explores Puget Sound and names Elliott Bay after a crewman.

1851
The Denny family of Illinois builds a cabin and starts one of the first successful non-Indian settlements in the Seattle area.

1856
A brief war breaks out between Native Americans and white settlers.

1866
Chief Sealth, who was always friendly to white settlers, dies. (One pronunciation of Chief Sealth's name is Seattle, and town leaders later adopted that name.)

1880
The population of Seattle is 3,553.

1886
Anti-Chinese riots break out in town.

1889
A fire caused by an overturned glue pot in a furniture factory burns 64 acres (26 ha) in downtown Seattle; an energetic rebuilding program begins immediately after the fire.

1897
Gold discovered in the Yukon triggers a gold rush, which draws thousands of people into the Seattle area.

1909
The Alaska-Yukon-Pacific Exposition attracts 3 million visitors to Seattle.

1916
Wealthy Seattle lumberman Bill Boeing builds his first airplane.

1919
A general strike, supported by nearly all working people, paralyzes the city.

1920
Seattle's population exceeds 300,000.

An arched red footbridge in Kubota Gardens

1940
The Mercer Island Floating Bridge is dedicated.

1941–1945
At the height of World War II, Boeing's Seattle-area plant completes 6,981 B-17 bombers before shifting production to the even larger B-29.

1954
Boeing announces plans to build its first jet passenger plane, the 707.

1962
The Century 21 Exposition opens, leaving the city with new structures such as the Pacific Science Center, the Space Needle, and the Opera House.

1977
The Seattle Mariners professional baseball team begins play.

1979
The Seattle SuperSonics, the city's pro basketball team, wins the National Basketball Association (NBA) championship.

1985
For the fourth year in a row, Seattle is rated the nation's number-one recreational city by an annual publication called *Vacation Places Rated Almanac*, published by the Rand McNally Company.

1989
Norman B. Rice becomes the city's first African-American mayor.

1992
A rare drought in the Seattle area forces citizens to cut water use dramatically.

1996
The Seattle SuperSonics reach the NBA finals, but are defeated by Michael Jordan and the Chicago Bulls.

SEATTLE

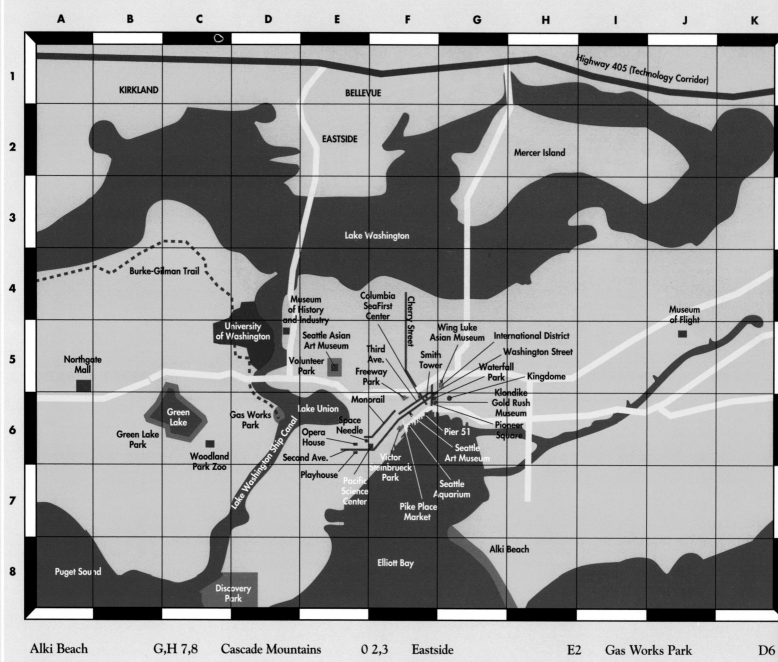

Map labels:

A B C D E F G H I J K (columns)
1 2 3 4 5 6 7 8 (rows)

Highway 405 (Technology Corridor)

KIRKLAND

BELLEVUE

EASTSIDE

Mercer Island

Lake Washington

Burke-Gilman Trail

Museum
of History
and Industry

University
of Washington

Columbia
SeaFirst
Center

Cherry Street

Wing Luke
Asian Museum

International District

Museum
of Flight

Seattle Asian
Art Museum

Third
Ave.

Smith
Tower

Washington Street

Northgate
Mall

Volunteer
Park

Freeway
Park

Waterfall
Park

Kingdome

Klondike
Gold Rush
Museum

Monorail

Green
Lake

Gas Works
Park

Lake Union

Space
Needle

Pioneer
Square

Green Lake
Park

Opera
House

Pier 51

Woodland
Park Zoo

Second Ave.

Seattle
Art Museum

Playhouse

Victor
Steinbrueck
Park

Seattle
Aquarium

Pacific
Science
Center

Pike Place
Market

Alki Beach

Puget Sound

Elliott Bay

Discovery
Park

Lake Washington Ship Canal

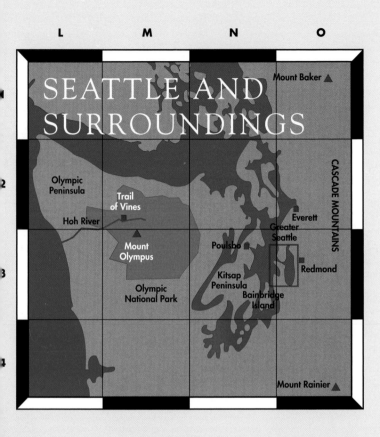

SEATTLE AND SURROUNDINGS

L   M   N   O

Mount Baker ▲

Olympic Peninsula

Trail of Vines

Hoh River

CASCADE MOUNTAINS

Everett
Greater Seattle

Poulsbo

Mount Olympus

Redmond

Kitsap Peninsula
Bainbridge Island

Olympic National Park

Mount Rainier ▲

GLOSSARY

conservatory: A greenhouse where plants are displayed

environs: Outskirts, nearby lands

ethnic: Pertaining to a nationality or religious group

hawkers: Noisy street sellers

jazz: A form of music that originated in the southern United States

landmark: An easily recognized building or land feature

legacy: A lesson or a philosophy handed down from the past

memorabilia: Objects that serve as a reminder of the past

metropolitan: Referring to cities

pontoons: Floating devices used on seaplanes

prevail: To be common, to dominate

raze: Dismantle or tear down

Scandinavian countries: Sweden, Norway, and Denmark

Picture Identifications

Cover: The skyline of downtown Seattle at dusk with Mount Rainier in the distance; employees at a vegetable stall in the Public Market
Page 1: A multi-racial Seattle family washing the family car
Pages 4-5: The Seattle skyline with Space Needle at dusk
Pages 8-9: Dining outside on the Seattle waterfront
Pages 20-21: Pioneer Square
Pages 30-31: Teenage girls participating in a Seattle Chinatown festival
Pages 44-45: Volunteer Park Conservatory and late summer gardens

INDEX

TO FIND OUT MORE

BOOKS

Bergman, Donna. *Seattle: A Fun-Packed, Fact-Filled, Travel & Activity Book*. Santa Fe, N.M.: John Muir Publications, 1996.

Dickinson, Joan D. *Bill Gates: A Billionaire Computer Genius*. Springfield, N.J.: Enslow Publishers, 1997.

Doherty, Craig A. and Katherine M. Doherty. *The Seattle Space Needle*. Building America series. Woodbridge, Conn.: Blackbirch Press, 1998

Fodor's Seattle and Vancouver. New York: Fodor's Travel Publications, 1998.

Fradin, Dennis B. *Washington*. From Sea to Shining Sea series. Chicago: Childrens Press, 1995.

Goodman, Michael E. *The History of the Seattle Mariners*. Mankato, Minn.: Creative Education, 1998.

Goodman, Michael E. *Seattle Seahawks*. Mankato, Minn.: Creative Education, 1997.

Goodman, Michael E. *Seattle SuperSonics*. Mankato, Minn.: Creative Education, 1998.

Snelson, Karin. *Seattle*. A Downtown America Book. New York: Dillon Press, 1992.

Steves, Rick. *Kidding Around Seattle: A Young Person's Guide to the City*. Santa Fe, N.M.: John Muir Publications, 1991.

ONLINE SITES

Seattle.com

http://www.seattle.com

Must-see sights, music, dining, maps, hotel information, movies.

Seattle Art Museum

http://www.seattleartmuseum.org/

Visit the museum's exhibits, learn about special events, read art essays, and drop in at the museum store.

Seattle Mariners

http://www.mariners.org

Club and player stats, rosters, schedules for the current baseball season, team history, and feature articles. Be sure to visit the Kids' Zone.

Seattle.net

http://www.seattle.net

Business, entertainment, and community information.

Seattle Public Access Network

http://www.ci.seattle.wa.us/

All kinds of useful information, including travel tips, weather forecasts, and news.

Seattle SuperSonics

http://www.nba.com/sonics/

The official site of Seattle's professional basketball team: player profiles, stats, ticket information, schedules, stories, photos. Also, send fan mail and shop in the NBA store.

Seattle Times

http://seattletimes.nwsource.com/

Link to Washington state's largest daily newspaper as well as to the *Seattle Post-Intelligencer*, which has been published continuously since 1863!

Space Needle

http://www.spaceneedle.com/

Visit Seattle's most famous landmark: history, photos, gift shop, and "Just for Kids."

ABOUT THE AUTHOR

R. Conrad Stein was born in Chicago. After serving in the U.S. Marines, he attended the University of Illinois where he earned a degree in history. He later studied in Mexico. Mr. Stein has published more than eighty history and geography books for young readers. He lives in Chicago with his wife and their daughter, Janna.

Traveling is Mr. Stein's passion. He has visited many cities in Europe, Latin America, Asia, and the United States. After a lifetime of traveling, he regards Seattle as one of his favorite towns.